Doberman Pinscher

Priyanka Das

My Dog

AV2
www.openlightbox.com

Step 1
Go to www.openlightbox.com

Step 2
Enter this unique code
ACHQYXF56

Step 3
Explore your interactive eBook!

Your interactive eBook comes with...

AV2 is optimized for use on any device

  Audio Listen to the entire book read aloud

 Videos Watch informative video clips

 Weblinks Gain additional information for research

 Try This! Complete activities and hands-on experiments

  Key Words Study vocabulary, and complete a matching word activity

 Quizzes Test your knowledge

 Slideshows View images and captions

 Share Share titles within your Learning Management System (LMS) or Library Circulation System

 Citation Create bibliographical references following APA, CMOS, and MLA styles

This title is part of our AV2 digital subscription

1-Year K–2 Subscription
ISBN 978-1-7911-3310-8

Access hundreds of AV2 titles with our digital subscription.
Sign up for a FREE trial at **www.openlightbox.com/trial**

The digital components of this book are guaranteed to stay active for at least five years from the date of publication.

Doberman Pinscher

CONTENTS

- 2 Interactive eBook Code
- 4 Brave and Alert
- 6 Large Dogs
- 8 Coat Colors
- 10 Growing Up
- 12 Guard Dogs
- 14 Exercise
- 16 Grooming
- 18 Food and Attention
- 20 Staying Healthy
- 22 Incredible Doberman Pinschers
- 24 Sight Words

My Doberman pinscher is brave and alert.

She is always ready to protect our home.

Dobermans are large, strong dogs. They are very fast and powerful.

Dog Shoulder Heights

German Shepherd
Up to 26 inches
(66 centimeters)

Doberman Pinscher
Up to 28 inches
(71 cm)

Great Dane
Up to 32 inches
(81 cm)

My Doberman has a shiny black coat with rust markings.

Some Dobermans have red, blue, or fawn coats with rust markings.

Doberman puppies are lively and energetic.

They learn quickly and should be trained early.

Where in the World

Doberman pinschers were first bred in Germany in the late 1800s.

Dobermans are protective of their families. They make good guard dogs.

Some are trained to protect people and places.

My Doberman is very active.

She needs more exercise than most dogs.

I brush my Doberman's short fur often.

This keeps her coat smooth and healthy.

I feed my Doberman twice a day.

She also needs plenty of attention and affection.

I take my Doberman to the veterinarian at least once a year.

The veterinarian helps keep my dog healthy.

Dog Breed Popularity in the United States

#14
Cavalier King Charles Spaniel

#15
Doberman Pinscher

#16
Cane Corso

20

Incredible Doberman Pinschers

Dobermans were bred to be **guard dogs** by a tax collector named **Karl Friedrich Louis Dobermann**.

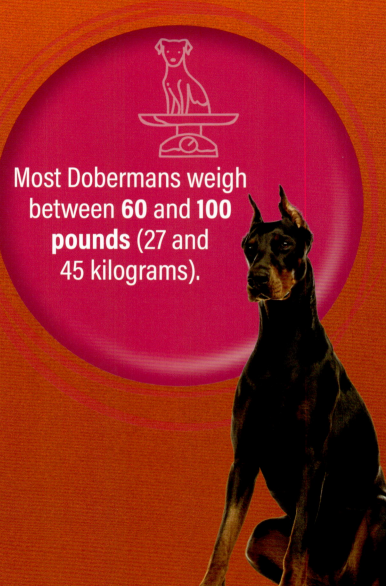

Most Dobermans weigh between **60** and **100 pounds** (27 and 45 kilograms).

Dobermans are **fast runners**, reaching speeds up to **35 miles** (56 kilometers) **per hour**.

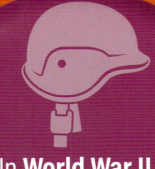

In **World War II**, the Doberman was the official **war dog** of the **U.S. Marine Corps**.

SIGHT WORDS

Research has shown that as much as 65 percent of all written material published in English is made up of 300 words. These 300 words cannot be taught using pictures or learned by sounding them out. They must be recognized by sight. This book contains 58 common sight words to help young readers improve their reading fluency and comprehension. This book also teaches young readers several important content words, such as proper nouns. These words are paired with pictures to aid in learning and improve understanding.

Page	Sight Words First Appearance
4	always, and, home, is, my, our, she, to
6	are, great, large, they, up, very
9	a, has, have, or, some, with
11	be, first, in, late, learn, should, the, were, where, world
12	good, make, of, people, places, their
14	more, most, needs, than
15	day, every, for, go, runs, we
17	her, I, keeps, often, this
19	also
20	at, helps, once, states, take, year

Page	Content Words First Appearance
4	Doberman pinscher
6	dogs, German shepherd, great Dane, heights, shoulder
9	coat, markings
10	puppies
11	Germany
12	families
14	exercise
17	fur
19	affection, attention
20	breed, cane corso, Cavalier King Charles spaniel, popularity, United States, veterinarian

Published by Lightbox Learning Inc.
276 5th Avenue, Suite 704 #917
New York, NY 10001
Website: www.openlightbox.com

Copyright ©2026 Lightbox Learning Inc.
All rights reserved. No part of this publication may be reproduced, stored in a retrieval system, or transmitted in any form or by any means, electronic, mechanical, photocopying, recording, or otherwise, without the prior written permission of the publisher.

Library of Congress Control Number: 2024057197

ISBN 979-8-8745-2138-7 (hardcover)
ISBN 979-8-8745-2139-4 (softcover)
ISBN 979-8-8745-2140-0 (static multi-user eBook)
ISBN 979-8-8745-2142-4 (interactive multi-user eBook)

012025
100924

Printed in Guangzhou, China
1 2 3 4 5 6 7 8 9 0 29 28 27 26 25

Project Coordinator: Priyanka Das
Designer: Jean Faye Rodriguez

Every reasonable effort has been made to trace ownership and to obtain permission to reprint copyright material. The publisher would be pleased to have any errors or omissions brought to its attention so that they may be corrected in subsequent printings.

The publisher acknowledges Getty Images and Shutterstock as its primary image suppliers for this title.